EMPOWERMENT
AND ATIYOGA

૭ଚ   ୦୫

BY TONY DUFF
PADMA KARPO TRANSLATION COMMITTEE

First edition, April 2006
Second edition, January 2010
ISBN: 978-9937-8244-5-3

Garamond typeface with diacritical marks
Designed and created by Tony Duff
Tibetan Computer Company
http://www.tibet.dk/tcc

Produced, Printed, and Published by
Padma Karpo Translation Committee
P.O. Box 4957
Kathmandu
NEPAL

Web-site and e-mail contact through:
http://www.tibet.dk/pktc
or search Padma Karpo Translation Committee on the web.

CONTENTS

CONTENTS

THE MEANING OF EMPOWERMENT IN GENERAL AND IN RELATION TO THE MAHA ATI SYSTEM IN PARTICULAR

RIPENING AND LIBERATING

The process of the Vajra Vehicle in Buddhism is summed up as twofold "ripening and liberating". Ripening refers to a process of maturing one's being in preparation for the actual process of liberating it. Liberation, done on the basis of the ripening empowerment, is the application of the specific techniques that liberate you from your samsaric style of being into an enlightened style of being.

Ripening is done using the technique called "empowerment". Empowerment consists of four major steps in the Buddhist tradition, each of which is a specific type of empowerment. The end result of being taken through the four steps of empowerment is that you have been shown all aspects of your being in their enlightened form.

This demonstration through empowerment of the enlightened side of the various aspects of your being plants a seed in your experience which can then be nurtured into the full-blown form, the full enlightenment of a truly complete buddha. Thus, empowerment is called the "doorway" and also the "gateway" to the vajra vehicle journey. You have to go through the departure gate at an airport otherwise you cannot go on the flight and, similarly, you have to be entered into and ripened within the mandala of a deity before you can take your seat on the vajra jet-liner in which you fly through the space of reality as the first class deity.

Once you have been entered and ripened through the process of empowerment, you are given the actual techniques of the Vajra Vehicle which you then use to liberate yourself from cyclic existence. In this way, the Vajra Vehicle is a process of ripening and liberating, with empowerment being the means for ripening and the actual practice of the techniques of the system being the means for actual liberation.

EMPOWERMENT

"Empowerment" was originally called "abhisheka" in India. It is none other than the process of coronation of a king. As with Europe, India used to be a collection of fiefdoms ruled by kings and there was a process of coronation for the king which put the king-to-be on the seat of rulership and invested in him the power to rule over his particular realm. These coronation ceremonies whether European or Indian relied on a universal set of principles: the king-to-be is put on his seat in a ceremony of pomp and circumstance; is introduced to the beings of his new realm, from consort, down through ministers, even to the most menial subjects in the distant corners of his realm; is given the sceptres that represent his particular power; and, finally, is anointed as a king with specially consecrated water.

Tibetan Buddhist texts that discuss the process of empowerment say that the Indian word "abhisheka" means "scattering and pouring". Some commentaries say that scattering means scattering obstacles to enlightenment and so comes to mean "destroying". However, scattering can also be understood to mean "sprinkling" water as part of the coronation and some teachers explain it that way. In fact, the word "abhisheka" when used in ancient India, and now, too, means "coronation" or other rite of ascension to power in which anointment with water is a hallmark of the ceremony involved. In short, just as we Europeans speak of coronation, the Indians speak of abhisheka.

In Buddhist practice, the process of being empowered into the vajra vehicle is consistent with the worldly procedure of crowning a king. You, as a potential deity, are made into the deity, put on your throne, and introduced to your realm. Following that, you are given your various sceptres of power and are, usually, sprinkled with consecrated water to complete the coronation. Of course, the empowerment ceremonies of Buddhist tantra are not mere replicas of the coronation ceremonies of worldly kings. The actual process of empowerment in Buddhist tantra is the process of putting a practitioner on the throne of enlightenment. This has two parts to it: first the practitioner has to be introduced to the enlightened realm of the deity concerned, then has to have his raw, un-enlightened body, speech, and mind matured into an enlightened body, speech, and mind. This two-fold process, which sums up the meaning of empowerment, is called "entering and ripening". The disciple is entered into the mandala by the vajra master then has his samsaric body, speech, and mind ripened into its inherent, enlightened body, speech, and mind.

Entrance into the mandala of the deity is the first step. The main step, following it, of ripening, is done in a series of four steps called the four empowerments. These steps correspond to the fact that, as a human being, you have body, speech, mind, and a pure thread that runs through all of that but which is covered over by delusion. The four empowerments address each of those aspects in that order, which is a sequence of going progressively from coarse to subtle.

The first empowerment is called the vase empowerment. It deals with the obscurations of the outer or body level of existence, which includes all of the physical senses and the world that we have based on those senses. The empowerment ripens your five, ordinary aggregates into their inherently pure aspects and plants the seed for future attainment of the physical form body of a buddha, the nirmanakaya.

The second empowerment is called the secret empowerment. It deals with the obscurations of the subtle body within the physical body. It ripens the subtle body into its pure form, which is particularly connected with primordial sound. Because of that, this empowerment is where you are given the mantra of the deity. The empowerment plants the seed for the future attainment of the subtle form body of a buddha, the sambhoga-kaya.

The third empowerment is called the prajnajnana empowerment. It deals with the obscurations of mind. It uses a consort, which is the prajna part of the name, to lead the disciple, through unification of masculine and feminine principles, to the wisdom of a buddha, which is the jnana part of the name; hence it is called the prajnajnana empowerment. The empowerment ripens mind into the luminosity aspect of the essence of mind. It plants the seed for the future attainment of the dharmakaya.

Plate 1. Wall mural at Dzogchen Monastery, east Tibet.
The mural shows Jigmey Lingpa.
Picture by the author, 2007.

The fourth empowerment is called the word or precious word empowerment. It uses words or other signals to point to reality as it is, which is the thread that runs through all experience, both enlightened and un-enlightened. It matures the entire being into the rigpa-emptiness which is the ultimate reality that marks all things. It plants the seed for the future attainment of the svabhavikakaya.

As mentioned earlier, empowerment ripens your being so that you could fully liberate yourself by the practices to be done following empowerment. Thus, there is the question of whether or not liberation also can occur within the ripening of empowerment. Liberation, to a greater or lesser extent, can occur within empowerment. However, the extent to which this happens, if it happens at all, is dependent on a variety of factors, especially the capacity of the disciple. For most of us, liberation happens because we go through the coronation ceremony that fully invests us with the right to be the deity and then we practise consistently until liberation—which is the full manifestation of our capabilities and activities as a king of all existence—is obtained. However, for those rare few individuals who have already journeyed sufficiently down the spiritual path so are ready vessels, significant amounts of liberation can occur within the empowerment ceremony itself.

Padma Karpo, of the Drukpa Kagyu, says,

> "Discursive thought[1] is a non-wisdom-mode thought of body, speech, and mind that generates the four circumstances—waking, dreaming, sleeping, and the fourth one[2]—which, since it binds tightly into samsara, is like a seal-knot. The empowerments outer, inner, secret, and ultimate—outer vase empowerment, inner secret empowerment, secret prajnajnana empowerment, and the ultimate fourth

empowerment—cause the seal of the knot of discursive thought to collapse. The way the collapse occurs is through "the essence of mind self-liberated": when the essence of mind, which is as-it-is, is communicated with, then discursive thought, which is not-as-it-is, collapses; it is like knowing the truth causes the collapse of falsity."

The Four Empowerments in Relation to Levels of Practice in the Vajra Vehicle

There are various levels of practice in the Vajra Vehicle. The highest ones are called Mahamudra and Maha Ati (which is most commonly called these days by its Tibetan name Dzogchen or its English name Great Completion). Both of these practices are typified as practices that focus on the meaning of the fourth level of empowerment; as is said,

"The fourth is the precious word empowerment. In it, all degradations and obscurations of body, speech, and mind, taken all together, are cleared off simultaneously. By it, you are empowered to practice vajra wisdom—Mahamudra and Maha Ati— that is, rigpa-emptiness. Having received it, you have planted a seed so that you are worthy to obtain the svabhavikakaya."

All four empowerments are necessary for all levels of Vajra Vehicle practice because each of the empowerments addresses a specific aspect of being. Thus, saying that the practices of Mahamudra and Maha Ati focus on the fourth empowerment does not mean that empowerments in their systems of practice only have the fourth empowerment in them. They do have all four empowerments and all four are needed and properly represented. What it means is that the liberating part, the actual practice of the main techniques of the system itself, focusses on the meaning that is shown in the fourth empowerment rather than in the first to third empowerments. Therefore, for those who intend to practice these systems, the fourth empowerment is of special interest.

Other types of practice focus on other levels of the four empowerments and those empowerments then become of special interest to people who are doing those practices. For example, all development stage practices focus on the meaning of the first empowerment. However, again, it is not that one empowerment is of interest to the exclusion of the others. Rather, all four are important and needed, but one might be of special interest.

Therefore, the next chapter in this book is the root empowerment of Great Completion as found in the Longchen Nyingthig transmission of Great Completion. There are many empowerments in the Longchen Nyingthig system but there is one which is the root of all of them. It is the first empowerment in the original *Root Volumes of the Longchen Nyingthig* and is the base empowerment of the whole set of empowerments contained in those volumes. This type of empowerment is special to the Maha Ati system and is called "The King's Coronation Anointing Vase" empowerment. It empowers a practitioner into the Great Completion view and, as such, is the root of all other empowerments in the transmission. The text of the empowerment is very short, making it an easy-to-understand overview of the procedure of empowerment in this system. Several of the verses used in the empowerment are used throughout the set of empowerments, for example, the lines used to accept the samayas at the end of the empowerment are used repeatedly in the other empowerments of the transmission.

Following that, two fourth empowerment texts taken from the empowerment texts of the Nyingma Kama transmission are presented. They were chosen because they present the fourth empowerment very clearly. The first is the most important of the Eight Logos empowerments—*The Narrow Fortress of The Eight Logos*—of the Nyingma Kama transmission. It is very similar to the root empowerment of the Longchen Nyingthig transmission and helps illustrate fourth empowerment principles—which is the meaning of Maha Ati—very clearly. The second is called a suchness empowerment but this is just another name for fourth empowerment. It is from one of the Red Yamantaka empowerments contained in the Nyingma Kama. This text is less explicit about the meaning of fourth empowerment than the first but helps to amplify on the principles involved. I have written copious notes for these two texts and these should help you to understand further the idea of the king's ascension at the Ati level. In addition, the Eight Logos empowerment text gives an especially nice introduction, in words, to the nature of mind that can inform and help your practice, especially of the Thorough Cut[3].

As mentioned above, ripening empowerment is the gateway to the vajra vehicle journey. After ripening empowerment has been received, you must obtain the liberating instructions and then, by practising them, liberate yourself. The Great Completion practice that corresponds to the two empowerment texts contained in here is the Thorough Cut. Therefore, I have included a practical instruction from Dilgo Khyentse Rinpoche on it. The instruction comes in the form of a letter written to one of his lady disciples. It is short but contains all the features of the path of the Thorough Cut. Rabjam Rinpoche taught the text to the disciples who gathered at Bodhgaya for the annual Zhechen retreat there in 2005.

There are two main practices in Maha Ati. The first is the Thorough Cut whose ripening empowerment and liberating instructions for practice are contained in here, as just mentioned. In addition to the Thorough Cut, there is also the practice of Direct Crossing. This practice requires its own, specific type of empowerment, called "The Empowerment of the Liveliness of Rigpa"[4]. Once that empowerment has been obtained, the liberating instructions of Direct Crossing can be received and practised. This level of empowerment is included in the root empowerment of the Longchen Nyingthig system found in the next chapter. It is mentioned in one line of the fourth empowerment. However, it is not very explicit. To receive the empowerment explicitly, there are several methods. In the Longchen Nyingthig system, the empowerment is contained within the famous text called *Written Instruction called Wisdom Guru*[5]. Alternatively, it is presented extensively in the empowerments of the Nyingthig Yazhi, which are connected with Longchen Nyingthig.

SOURCES OF THE EMPOWERMENT TEXTS: NYINGMA KAMA AND LONGCHEN NYINGTHIG

The Vajra Vehicle dharma that originally came into Tibet with Padmasambhava, Vairochana, and Vimalamitra is maintained by the Tibetan Buddhist tradition called "Nyingma". Nyingma simply means "The Early System" and the name is given to set it off from the other systems that came later and were called "newer" systems. Nyingma is sometimes translated as "The Ancient Ones" but that is not really the meaning. Maha Ati is the ultimate teaching within the Nyingma tradition and accordingly, all of the texts here are from the Nyingma system.

The Vajra Vehicle teachings of the Nyingma were transmitted down through time in two main ways. They were transmitted directly from one person to another in a long succession of transmission; this is called "Kama"[6] meaning "the word". And they were transmitted by being concealed and then recovered at some later time in a short succession of transmission; this is called "Terma"[7] meaning "treasure".

This book uses texts of both Kama and Terma. There are two empowerment texts from the Nyingma Kama collection and there is the root empowerment text from the Longchen Nyingthig collection. The Nyingma Kama is a collection of all the empowerments that have been transmitted from one person to another since Padmasambhava and his associates. There are various forms of this collection, because there have been different compilations made by various Tibetan masters. All of them are very large collections. The latest one, by Dudjom Rinpoche, numbers ninety-six volumes.

Longchen Nyingthig is the name given to the transmission of the teachings that came down to us from Longchen Rabjam through Jigmey Lingpa—who is considered to be an emanation of Longchen Rabjam—as a type of Terma. Jigmey Lingpa received the teachings in a series of visions and direct mental revelations so they are called "Mind Terma". These teachings, which are of the most ultimate Maha Ati, were collectively called Longchen Nyingthig. They were written down and included in the collected works of Jigmey Lingpa which occupy fourteen volumes in total. Of them, three volumes are filled with the Longchen Nyingthig revelations and accordingly are called *The Root Volumes of the Longchen Nyingthig*[8]. These volumes start with three texts by Jigmey Lingpa that tell the story of how he received the teachings, which are followed by the texts for giving the empowerments of the transmissions and various sadhanas and liturgies for performing the practices.

Since that time, many other writings concerning Longchen Nyingthig have appeared, coming from various great gurus. Some of these writings directly concern the original transmission that was received by Jigmey Lingpa and in recent times these have been gathered together and put into additional volumes of teachings that are now included with the original, three *Root Volumes of the Longchen Nyingthig*. There was one extra volume to start with and now, in the latest print, there are two extra volumes making a five volume set. The extra material in the additional volumes is comprised of lineage prayers, sadhanas for the deities in Longchen Nyingthig that were received in visions, some commentaries on the practices, an explanation of an alternative sequence for the empowerments, and other, similar materials. The extra material in the additional volumes comes mainly from the first and third incarnations of Dodrupchen Rinpoche (there are various listings of the main disciples of Jigmey Lingpa but, generally speaking, the two main ones were Jigmey Thrinley Ozer, who became the first Dodrupchen Rinpoche, and Jigmey Gyalway Nyugu, who was one of Patrul Rinpoche's gurus). There is also a significant amount of material from Khyentse Wangpo, the first Khyentse Rinpoche. There are several items from Dilgo Khyentse Rinpoche. There are a couple of commentaries by two great khenpos of the tradition.

In the winter of 2005, Zhade'u Thrulzhig Rinpoche bestowed the Nyingma Kama Dilgo Khyentse and Dudjom Rinpoche's incarnations together with a large assembly at Zhechen Monastery, Kathmandu, Nepal. Then in April, 2006, he bestowed the Longchen Nyingthig empowerments on a similar audience. I made a variety of translations during these empowerments in order to assist the Western students who were there.

It culminated in this book which was put together in order to clarify the meaning of empowerment in general but especially in relation to Maha Ati, the ultimate teaching of the tradition that was being passed on.

Rabjam Rinpoche, who captains Zhechen Monastery, said to me recently that he appreciated the production of this type of translation and commentary for the sake of participants at Zhechen programs. As he said, it gives them something to take with them. It is immensely gratifying to please such a great hero of the teaching, of course. My real hope though is that it will open the door to empowerment in general for Western students and in particular to the wisdom of the fourth empowerment as the basis for the entire Ati journey.

OUR SUPPORTS FOR STUDY

I have been encouraged over the years by all of my teachers and gurus to pass on some of the knowledge I have accumulated in a lifetime dedicated to the study and practice, primarily through the Tibetan Buddhist tradition, of Buddhism. On the one hand they have encouraged me to teach. On the other hand, they are concerned that, while many general books on Buddhism have been and are being published, there are few books that present the actual texts of the tradition. They and many other, closely involved people have encouraged me to make and publish high quality translations of individual texts of the tradition.

In general, we have published a wide range of books that present the important literature of Tibetan Buddhism. In particular, this book is about one of the central features of the most profound systems of teaching that came into Tibet—Mahamudra and Great Completion—and we have published many of the important texts of these systems, with each one carefully selected to inform about a particular aspect of that teaching. As a follow on from this to the Mahamudra teaching, you would find our book *Gampopa's Mahamudra, the Five-Part Mahamudra of the Kagyus* to be very useful reading. Also, a forthcoming publication which contains Gampopa's interviews with his main yogi disciples, including the first Karmpa, focusses on the central issue of the meaning of fourth empowerment—rigpa—in the Kagyu teaching of Essence Mahamudra, and this also would be good reading. On the Great Completion side, we have a wide variety of books both more general, such as *Hinting At Dzogchen*, and more specialized texts of the tradition, too numerous to mention here though *Alchemy of Accomplishment* by Dudjom Rinpoche would be a very helpful read.

All in all, you will find many books both for free and for sale on our web-site, all of them prepared to the highest level of quality. Many of our books are available not only on paper but as electronic editions that can be downloaded, and all of them are prepared to the highest level of quality. We encourage you to look at our web-site to see what we have; the address is on the copyright page at the front of this book. Major book sellers also carry our paper editions.

It has also been a project of ours to make tools that non-Tibetans and Tibetans alike could use for the study and translation of Tibetan texts. As part of that project, we prepare electronic editions of Tibetan texts in the Tibetan Text input office of the Padma Karpo Translation Committee and make them available to the world. Tibetan texts are often corrupt so we make a special point of carefully correcting our work before making it available through our web-site. Thus, our electronic texts are not careless productions like most Tibetan texts found on the web but are highly reliable editions that can be used by non-scholars and scholars alike. Moreover, many of the texts are free. The Tibetan texts for this book are not available from us at the moment. We will shortly be making the entire set of the Root Volumes of Longchen Nyingthig available and that will contain the first text of this book. The text of Dilgo Khyentse Rinpoche's advice found at the end of the book can be obtained from his Collected Works. The remaining texts can be obtained from any of the Nyingma Kama Collections.

Our electronic texts can be read, searched, and so on, using our Tibetan software. The software can be used to set up a reference library of these texts and then used to read and even research them quickly and easily. The software, called TibetD and TibetDoc, has many special features that make it useful not only for reading but also for understanding and even translating texts. One key feature is that you can highlight a Tibetan term in a text then look it up immediately in any of our electronic dictionaries. We suggest the highly acclaimed *Illuminator Tibetan-English Dictionary* as the best dictionary for the purpose. As with all of our publications, the software and electronic texts can be obtained from our web-site whose address is on the copyright page at the front of the book.

Lotsawa Tony Duff,
Bauddha
Nepal
January, 2010

ༀ From Longchen Nyingthig:

The Root Empowerment, "The King's Coronation Anointing Vase Empowerment"

I bow to self-knowing, the factual deity.

The great secret vajra vehicle
Has for its entrance empowerment whose life-force is samaya
And for its nature actuality which is inexpressible;
Thus, in order to accept disciples of supreme fortune,
The base empowerment, The King's Coronation Anointing
    Vase is presented.
SAMAYA

In an excellent place, isolated and pleasant,
Nicely set up the mandala which will form the basis.
In the centre, set a ratna vase
With mouth ornamentation and neck ties, filled with liquid.
To the right, put this text as the volume and
To the left, put the secret substance bhañja.
Above it, put a mirror with sindhura,
A Vajrasatva mirror[9], and
The family chakali[10] with a canopy erected over it.
Expel the obstructors. Do the activities according to

15

Rigdzin Dupa's text and practise the capable one.
With samadhi, arise through self-entry[11].
Have the disciples sit in the rows.
Wash them with water from the activity vase. Banish the
    obstructors.
Meditate on a protection circle then explain the history.
Have them offer a mandala and supplicate:

HOḤ
I, a fortunate son of the family
Have been accepted by the great compassionate one;
Please enter and ripen me
In the great samaya mandala.

Have them request with that three times then give the reply:

HOḤ
In this the supreme of secret's mandalas,
Difficult to enter and of high rewards with high risks
Because all is lost if samaya is corrupted,
An empowerment in which the samaya is to be kept will
    be given.

Having announced that, impart the vows of refuge and
    bodhichitta.
Perform an accumulation of virtue with the seven limbs.
Through that, they become a suitable basis for the
    empowerment.
After that, the son disciples[12] are generated as the deity then
The descent of wisdom is done assiduously.
Seal with TIṢHṬHA VAJRA and
Empower by placing the vase on the crown:

HŪṂ
The auspicious vase, the deity's immeasurable palace and
The water of amrita non-dual with the deity

Empower the fortunate son through which
Attachment to appearances is finished as the symbol, the
    deity's body.
You attain Full-Maturation Vidyadhara[13];
Come and tread upon the Total Light level.
root mantra and KĀYA ABHIṢHIÑCHA OM

The secret substance[14] is placed at the Bliss-Protector[15] throat:

HŪṂ
The red and white bodhicittas of male and female uniting
Swirl together inside the bhandha[16].
The fortunate son is empowered through which
The channel constituents'[17] letters are fully ripened.
You attain Control-Over-Life Vidyadhara;
Come and tread upon the Padma-Containing level.
root mantra and VĀK ABHIṢHIÑCHA ĀḤ

Place a fully qualified consort[18] in his hand:

HŪṂ
The source of all dharmas,
The great-bliss woman, the secret's consort[19],
Is given to the son of the family through which
The wisdoms of the four joys are manifest.
You attain Mahamudra Vidyadhara;
Come and tread upon the Great Assemblage of Wheel
    level.
root mantra and CITTA ABHIṢHIÑCHA HŪṂ

Show, on top of a bell-metal, circular mirror,
The Vajrasatva mirror:

HOḤ
Alpha purity mirror, the pure portal[20], and
Spontaneous-existence crystal, clarity without stains[21]—

By the empowerment completed through symbolic signs
Stainless rigpa's actuality is realized.
You attain Spontaneous-existence Vidyadhara;
Come and tread upon the Great Bliss level.
root mantra and DHARMADHĀTU ABHIṢHIÑCHA HŪṂ

Give them the factual introduction to actuality[22]*:*
Rest equipoised in the state free from extremes;
Saying, "PHAṬ", separate mind and rigpa;
Saying, "AḤ", give the reality introduction.

Then entrust the command with the volume.

HOḤ
Dharmakaya Samantabhadra,
Sambhogakaya five conqueror families,
Nirmanakaya Garab Dorje,
Acharya Manjushrimitra,
Vidyadhara Shri Singha,
Mahapandita Vimalamitra,
Uddiyana Padma Thothreng,
Dakini Yeshe Tsogyal,
Sovereign Trisong Deutsen,
Conqueror's son Drimey Ozer[23],
Longchen Namkha'i Yogin[24], and so on—
the Nature Great Completion's glorious guardian
vidyadhara root together with lineage gurus, ocean of
yidams and dakinis, and assembly of oceans of samaya-
bound dharmapalas all together, please here, today,
empower the vajra disciples. Please bless them. Please
make their realization blaze. Please rouse their yogic
activity. You who have already attained the seat of
rulership that goes with the mind of the space of Great
Completion freed from the activities and efforts of rational
mind, please act so that they obtain in one life and one

body, the rainbow body, the supreme body of great transferrence, setting them at the rank of glorious Samantabhadra.

Say that three times and transfer the factual lineage[25].
Set the consciousness in a state without aim.

Then give the order of samaya by
Explaining the divisions and having them repeat them.
The root samayas—supreme body, speech, and mind,
The branches—twenty five,
And non-existent, solely, openness, and so on[26],
You must keep according to the ritual text.

Say that then have them offer a mandala in return for what has been given.

And again, in order to proclaim obedience as servants:

Whatever the leader commands
All that I will do.

Have them say that three times, then dedicate the merit.
SAMAYA.
This is all.

ॐ ॐ

Translated by Lotsawa Tony Duff on the occasion of the Longchen Nyingthig empowerments at Zhechen Monastery, April 2006.

appear on the ordinary person's consciousness. Therefore, it is superfactual the holy, but more literally? What this wisdom sees is true for the beings who have it, therefore what the wisdom sees is superfactual truth.

Superfactual truth, Skt. paramārthasatya, Tib. don dam bden pa. See under "Superfactual" for an explanation of this term.

Thorough Cut, Tib. khregs chod; the Dzogchen system has several levels to it. The innermost level has two main practices, the first called Thregcho, which literally translates as Thorough Cut and the second called Thogal which translates as Direct Crossing. The meaning of Thorough Cut has been misunderstood. The meaning is clearly explained in the *Illuminator Tibetan-English Dictionary*:

> Thorough Cut is a practice in which the solidification that sentient beings produce by having rational minds, which grasp at a perceived object and perceiving subject, is sliced through so as to get the underlying reality which has always been present in the essence of mind, and which is called Alpha Purity in this system of practice. Successful Thorough Cut is also known as "Alpha Purity Thorough Cut."

The syllable khregs chod is explained in the Dzogchen teachings either as ཁྲེགས་ཆོད or འཁྲེགས་ཆོད. In either case, the term ཆོད is "a cut". There are all sorts of different cuts and this is one of them. Then in the case of ཁྲེགས it is an adverb modifying the verb "to cut" and has the meaning of making the cut fully, completely. It is explained with the example of slicing off a finger. A finger could be sliced with a sharp knife such that the cut was not quite complete and the cut off portion was left hanging. Alternatively, it could be sliced through in one decisive movement such that the finger was completely and definitely severed. That kind of thorough cut

FROM THE COLLECTED NYINGMA KAMA: THE FOURTH EMPOWERMENT OF THE NARROW FORTRESS OF THE EIGHT LOGOS

Prostrations to glorious Samantabhadra!

Next, the empowerment-general[27] of the view of the vehicles
Is conferral of empowerment of the four intents of the
*   authentic view[28].*
The master draws a white letter A on the palm of his hand
And rests his mind in the uncontrived dharmata[29].
The disciple's hand takes hold of a precious jewel.
The master with consort and disciple with consort,
Are evident as the form of the dharmakaya Samantabhadra
*   with consort.*

HŪṂ
All is spontaneous existence[30], Samantabhadra's
    phenomena,
Their nature is absence of elaboration[31], Samantabhadri's
    state,
The two non-dual is the king of methods which runs
    throughout[32],
The two non-dual is the dharmadhatu conferral of
    empowerment[33].

Samantabhadri, the self-arisen bhagavat,
Is the abiding-only-in-dharmadhatu
One's-own-enlightened-mind deity;
Homage to the deity that is superfactual mind![34]

*Then, the master places his right hand on the disciple's head
and says:*

HŪM̐
Samantabhadra, stainlessness's
Universal governor, shines forth as the wisdom king[35];
Your own mind's complete purity[36], shines forth as
    concept's king[37];
Enlightenment's essence shines forth as great bliss[38];
Everything without exception is the spontaneous existence
    of dharmakaya;
All phenomena are contained within your own mind;
Since mind's personage[39] is nothing whatsoever,
Since the bindu's nature is absence of elaboration,
The equality king governs over all;
The very complete king of dharmata rigpa,
That shows each without mixup is the supreme of
    vehicles[40].
These with none missed[41] are to be swiftly completed for
    which reason
There is the supreme empowerment of view, the King's
    Coronation Anointing Vase and by conferring it
May you have the kingship of coronation via the all-
    encompassing supreme empowerment[42].

OM̐ SARVA TATHĀGATA SALAPATRAPUTERACANA ŚHVA
    SVABHĀVA ATMAKO 'HAM

By conferral of the King's Coronation Anointing Vase
    empowerment,

May you realize glorious Samantabhadra's intent from the
    depths and so
Obtain the empowerment of dharmata Great
    Completion[43]!

*Next, the conferral of the view empowerment. Have the
disciple stare penetratingly into the space in front:*

HŪM
Look, look, you fortunate one!
Look at this space before you!
In the luminosity crystal-clarity devoid of extremes
Is the absence of grasping to any position—this
Is the view freed from the extremes of falling into sides.
Remaining in this fact[44]
Is the intent[45] of the buddhas of the three times.

Oh child of the family! In this space before you, where
there is no colour or shape, this luminosity which is
unobstructed, empty openness freed of the extremes of
existing and not-existing, this absence of any and every
grasping whatsoever, the view divorced from the extremes
of falling into sides, is the intent of the buddha; recognize
it![46]

Those were the words of the introduction.

Next, the conferral of the meditation empowerment:

HŪM
Look, look, you fortunate one!
Look within at your own mind!
In the luminosity[47] no concepts, no distraction;
Like a lamp unshaken by wind
Meditation is self-illumination[48], without grasping.
Always meditate on this fact!

It is the intent of the buddhas.

O, child of the family! Fortunate one! When you look
within at your own mind: in mind there are no things or
conceptual tokens[49]; in the luminosity there are no
concepts, no distractions—it is unmoved by discursive
thoughts—so; like a lamp unshaken by wind, relax and rest
there! Just exactly this, meditation done as self-
illumination without grasping, is the buddha's intent, so
meditate always inseparable from it!

Those were the words of the introduction.

Next, the conferral of the fruition empowerment:

HŪṂ
Look, look, you fortunate one!
Look at the unchanging fact[50] of dharmakaya!
Beyond extremes of expression[51] through word or thought,
The state of emptiness in which nothing—
Just like water poured onto dough[52]—is established,
Is the no arising, no cessation dharmakaya;
Fruition is to have unchanging assurance[53].
You are to remain in this fact!
The buddhas of the three times remain in this.

*Say that and pour some bodhichitta combined with liquor
into the disciple's mouth, then,*

The fact of dharmata beyond words, thoughts, expressions
altogether; this empty nature, without the duality of
arising and cessation, is to be done as a fruition of having
unchanging assurance in the dharmakaya so, since all the
buddhas of the three times remain in this state, you are to
stay unchangeably in this fact!

Those were the words of the introduction.

Next, the conferral of the conduct empowerment:

HŪṂ

Listen, listen, you fortunate one!

In the play of self-arising wisdom,

The unobstructed king of methods

Conducts whatever appears as the deeds of buddha

And each being conducted in bliss, it is liberated in its own
    place.

The conduct-general which is without restriction,

Is the conduct of the intent of the buddhas of the three
    times.

O, child of the family! Fortunate one! The meaning of
the empowerment from head to toe has been summed up
into four topics of view, meditation, fruition, and conduct.
As it cannot be bestowed using another empowerment
more kingly than this, the view, meditation, fruition, and
conduct are at the limit and the foremost instructions[54] are
at full measure. Thus, buddha has self-arisen in the mind.
Thus, all vehicles of the precepts, outer and inner, and all
phenomena of samsara and nirvana come from nowhere
other than your own mind. Thus, the empowerment of
the view-general brings buddha devoid of good or bad; the
empowerment of the meditation-general brings abiding
without anything to meditate on or any meditation to do;
the empowerment of the fruition-general brings realization
of the non-duality of birth and death; and the
empowerment of the conduct-general brings remaining in
absence of bondage or liberation. Thus, for the four
empowerments of that sort, any yogin who hears them by
ear and who has them stay in mind obtains the
empowerment-general of the views of the vehicles. Thus,
since every empowerment stems from this, it is the
grandfather of all empowerments.

Thus, the introduction is given.

From the Vajramala, this is the twelfth chapter, the chapter on the view, meditation, fruition, and conduct empowerment-general of the vehicles.

Translated by Lotsawa Tony Duff on the occasion of the Nyingma Kama empowerments at Zhechen Monastery, November, 2004.

FROM THE COLLECTED NYINGMA KAMA:
THE SUCHNESS EMPOWERMENT OF
THE SIX-FACED YAMANTAKA

[The outer, inner, and secret empowerments of Six-Faced Yamantaka are given. Then the vajra master says:]
Having thus obtained the secret empowerment, it is now appropriate to receive the suchness empowerment, so repeat this supplication after me:

HOḤ
Teacher who is the Guiding Light, the Bhagavat;
Gods; and Master please consider me!
Please enter me into the mandala of rigpa bodhichitta
Via the self-liveliness of the five wisdoms.
Say that three times.

Then, the master and disciples both enter equipoise:
ĀḤ
In uncontrived dharma's complete purity,
Unsought, self-arising wisdom becomes
The equipoise, spontaneous presence, the fact of
    dharmakaya;
Rigpa's liveliness is the empowerment;

By it, may the Great Completion bodhichitta
    empowerment;
The ultimate supreme empowerment, be complete![55]
DHARMA PRAJÑĀ PAÑCA ABHIṢHIÑCA HOḤ

Self-arising wisdom—the nature co-emergent wisdom and
the similitude wisdom of melting bliss co-emergent
wisdom both inseparable—is like space, is absent of every
expression and past being an object of word and thought.
The liveliness of its rigpa shining forth in great variety; is
the essence of the five wisdoms appearing unhindered!
That moreover, being the bodhichitta with essence of bliss,
emptiness, and luminosity, is the enlightened body aspect,
Akshobhya; the unborn emptiness not being contaminated
with faults of conceptual structures is the speech aspect
Amitabha; that wisdom of inseparable bliss-emptiness
overcomes every one of grasped-grasping's concepts, so is
the mind aspect Vajrasatva; that mindness's wisdom of
great bliss is the source of every one of the buddha
qualities, so it is the qualities aspect, Ratnasambhava; it
liberates the concepts built on conceptual structures and
expands the buddha's wisdom, so it is the activity aspect,
Amoghasiddhi. Recognise the five aspects primordially
complete within yourself, this is the self-shining-forth,
great primordial liberation![56]

*The actual explanation that goes with this suchness
empowerment is not in the text as passed down so these root
verses of the empowerment should be supplemented with other
material, whatever is suitable.[57]*

ॐ   ॐ

Translated by Lotsawa Tony Duff on the occasion of the Nyingma Kama empowerments at Zhechen Monastery, November, 2004.

FROM THE COLLECTED WORKS OF DILGO KHYENTSE RINPOCHE: ADVICE TO A LADY DISCIPLE

In the land of Chamara on Glorious Mountain are
The father, all refuges embodied, the Lotus Born Lord and
The mother, queen of dakinis, Princess of Karchen;
I remember my gurus, the two inseparable[58].

Early and late, do your daily recitations, then
In between, if you can take a holiday, stay relaxed.
Look unswervingly at your own entity, the innate aspect
    of mind!
There are no dharmas showing there as things but
The totally relaxed openness brings ease to rational mind.
If you recognize that, it is Padma Jungnay.

It is all right not to have a big name or project though
Thinking that your mind is tough and unworkable is
    discursive thought[59].
The liveliness[60], discursive thought, freed from birth,
    cessation, and dwelling,
Is your basic disposition[61] like space; assume this, your
    natural seat, beyond harm!

Without a draught, a lamp is luminous—

Within that state, familiarize your mind with whichever of
The *Seven Topics of Mind Training*[62] are agreeable to you.
Then through love and compassion, all prayers of
    aspiration are obtained.
For speech, recitation of *The Good Conduct*[63] is excellent.

None of the migrator beings, high or low, in these times of
    residue[64]
Is not gripped by the negative forces that arise from karmic
    confusion[65].
Because of it, worlds and the beings within are filled with
    evil deeds.
If you tame your own mind, all dharmas, such as those,
    will be included[66].
In mind's appearances there is no existence but they are
    vivid indeed.
The complexion, the luminosity part, not stopped is
    transparency[67].
If you simply recognize it, well, that's enough!
Relaxing naturally in that, look without distraction!
When you have fully turned your thought to this,
There is, except for the bodies of man and woman, no
    difference between us!

Through knowledge of the key points[68], preserve in
    nakedness the reality of the basic disposition[69]!
Send all forms, good and bad, of mind's liveliness into self-
    liberation[70]!
For a bird, knowing as it does how to fly, the sky is easy;
Clouds and wind currents are not a bother.
For a fish, knowing as it does how to swim, the water is
    easy;
Why would thoughts of caution, due to worries of
    suffocation, arise?

For a yogin who knows how to meditate, everything is
     easy;
All objects and circumstances are rainbow-drawings in the
     midst of space!

Do not steer towards the appearances of mind's liveliness,
     instead, look at the basic disposition!
When you attain finality in regard to the basic disposition,
     that is dharmakaya!
May you attain manifest enlightenment in which
There is no distinction between glorious Samantabhadra,
     male and female[71]!

Written by Mangala.

❧   ❦

*Translated following the commentary given by Zhechen
Rabjam Rinpoche to the students at Zhechen Tennyi Ling's
winter seminar at the buddha's seat of enlightenment in the
aryan land, for the sake of the fellow practitioners by Lotsawa
Tony Duff, December 6th, 2005. May there be virtue!*

NOTES

1. The use of concepts as the way of relating to your world; this is the way of samsara.

2. Sexual union.

3. Tib. khregs chod.

4. Tib. rig pa'i rstal dbang.

5. Tib. khrid yig ye shes bla ma. The text is usually kept very private but an authoritative translation can be obtained from the author. Snow Lion published a translation of it in 2008 but it is seriously problematic; despite all the hype included in the text as a means of attesting to its correctness, it is mistaken in very many places and actually missing pieces of the text.

6. Tib. bka' ma.

7. Tib. gter ma. Although usually translated as "treasure", the actually meaning of "terma" is actually just "something that has been hidden away for later use".

8. Tib. klong chen nying thig rtsa pod.

9. A "Vajrasatva mirror" is actually a crystal. Together with the bronze mirror, it is used to give the fourth empowerment in all of

the Longchen Nyingthig empowerments.

10. Chakali is Sanskrit for "picture card"; it is saying to put the picture cards of the empowerment deity's family there.

11. The master who will give the empowerment first has to arise as the deity by empowering himself, which is called "self-entry".

12. This text was written with male practitioners in mind. It is not the translator's job to change the author's words; ladies can simply change the wording to fit.

13. This empowerment ripens a disciple in four stages by taking them through the four steps of realization of the Nyingma system, the four levels of Vidyadhara, meaning the four levels of people who have gained rigpa.

14. Carried in the kapala.

15. The name of the chakra inside the throat.

16. A bhandha is a skull cup.

17. The constituent of the body which is the channels through which the winds run.

18. A fully qualified consort is one who has all the characteristics needed for the practice of karmamudra. This third level of empowerment empowers the disciple to undertake karmamudra practice.

19. Often translated as "the secret consort" but it does not mean a consort who is kept secret, it means a consort of the secret, where secret is a name for the vajra path.

20. The mirror that represents alpha purity. Alpha purity is a key term of Thorough Cut practice. It points at the fundamental and primordial purity of mind, freed from all self-grasping, that the

practice leads to. This purity is the portal to being able to develop the spontaneous existence of the appearing aspect which is done with Direct Crossing practice.

21. The entirety of the view of Maha Ati is summed up in the two things of alpha purity (Tib. ka dag) and spontaneous existence (Tib. lhun grub). Alpha purity refers to the emptiness of the ground, which is therefore pure. Spontaneous existence refers to the appearances that come from the ground. The mirror and crystal are the signs that communicate the fact, which is reality described as alpha purity and spontaneous existence.

22. The fourth empowerment communicates the fact of reality through a symbolic sign. The introduction to the nature of mind shows that reality in fact, not through symbolic means. Actuality is a word meaning reality, as it actually is.

23. Longchen Rabjam.

24. Jigmey Lingpa.

25. The lineage of reality in fact, not a lineage of a conventional form of reality.

26. The first three of the four special samayas of Maha Ati. The fourth is spontaneously existent.

27. In general, the terminology of this empowerment is in the unique terminology of the Great Completion system. In particular, it is the specific terminology of the king's empowerment and the rulership over all that goes with it. The Great Completion is the very king of views. It not only rules over all lesser views but is contained within all of them, too, for they are just coarser expressions of this ultimate expression of reality. If you keep this in mind and read the text carefully, you will see a whole way of talking that corresponds to

the sovereignty of a king. It is like the terminology that you would encounter when speaking of the highest levels of government.

The dharmakaya kind of king, which is the king we are speaking of here, governs all phenomena, with no phenomenon excluded. Not only does it govern every phenomenon but it suffuses every phenomenon as well. Therefore, anything to do with this king is "general". For example, the empowerment of this king is not just any supreme empowerment but is the empowerment-general of all empowerments. Just as the secular world of government has the term "secretary-general" to mean the secretary over all secretaries, so the realm of this king has an empowerment-general; it is the empowerment of all empowerments, the most supreme empowerment that rules over and contains at once, all other empowerments.

In this system, the master brings his disciple, who is but yet a prince, to the level of being a king through empowerment. He uses the method of bringing the prince-in-waiting to the position of king. To bring someone to the position of king, there is the ceremony of coronation. In most cultures—including ancient India and Europe— coronation requires anointment which is done by sprinkling consecrated water on the head of the person being made a king. In the ancient Indian tradition, this process was called "abhiṣheka" which literally means "sprinkling and pouring" because it is the key feature of a king's coronation.

In a coronation, a special vessel of consecrated water is used to do the anointing. In the ancient traditions of India, ascetics had a vase that they kept with them as a water container. This vase had a particular name—a "kamandalu". It wasn't a coronation vase but just the vase that spiritual practitioners kept with them for water. Later, the vase became used in the Buddhist world. It was used by monks as their water vase. It also became the vase used for this kind of empowerment. Thus, this empowerment in Great Completion became known as the "King's Coronation Kamandalu empowerment".

I've translated it here as "King's Coronation Anointing Vase empowerment" though note that "anointing vase" is not what the name really means; it is the vase of a spiritual practitioner which was later pressed into use as the vase used to anoint a disciple.

You will find many other words in this text that belong to the language of sovereignty. If you look carefully and read and re-read the text, you will find all of the threads, I am sure. Words such as "universal" and "general" and "encompassing" are not accidental; they are part of the sovereignty of the king of the view of Great Completion.

Note that this is a very exacting translation of the original. There are very few things added to make it easy to understand. At the same time, I have deliberately retained some very unusual constructions of the original because they convey the meaning just as intended. If I were to have translated them into a more flowing style of English, the original meaning would have been lost.

This is not one of those texts that you can just pick up and read and understand. It contains the highest level of instructions of any of the Buddhist vehicles and with much of the specialized language of that vehicle. In addition, the text itself is not composed for simple reading. It requires a great deal of knowledge of the subject to make sense of it. So, if you do not understand it, it might be that you still need more instruction on the Thorough Cut. Or, even if you have had many instructions in that, try reading the text again and again to find the connections and the meaning.

28. In other words, the conferral of this empowerment-general will be performed here by conferring it in four empowerments, one each for view, meditation, fruition, and conduct.

29. A is the seed-syllable representing dharmata.

30. Tib. lhun grub. Spontaneous existence is a key term of Mahamudra and Maha Ati. It means existence that is not produced through causes and effects.

31. Tib. sprod pa med pa. Elaboration is the dualistic mind's mode of elaborating on non-conceptual reality using concepts.

32. The king of all methods is the Great Completion, which rules over but also is present throughout all lesser methods, that is, all of the lesser vehicles.

33. The two non-dual, that is, that kind of reality, is not only the king of methods but is also the means by which this empowerment is conferred.

34. Empowerments are usually about a deity. This verse sets Samantabhadri as the deity of the empowerment by pointing out that she is the deity never separated from ultimate reality and the one which is thus the symbol of one's own enlightened mind. In other words, you are being empowered into ultimate reality on the basis of the ultimate reality contained in your own mind and that is the deity of the empowerment.

That kind of deity, that kind of reality, is the so-called "absolute truth" level. "Relative" and "absolute" are quite incorrect; the actual terms are "fictional" and "superfactual" respectively; see the *Illuminator Tibetan-English Dictionary* for full explanation.

Fictional is like this: the term means the level of reality (*truth*) made up by the obscuration of an ordinary person's mind. Because this is an obscured version of actual truth it is *fictional*. However, it is true for the beings who make it up, so it is still called *truth*.

Superfactual is like this: the term means the level of reality (*truth*) that is seen by the wisdom of a being who has transcended samsara. This wisdom is *superior* to the ordinary person's consciousness and the *facts* that appear on its surface are *true* compared to the facts that appear to the mind in the fictional reality of the ordinary person.

35. Samantabhadra is the governor or ruler who belongs to, that is, comes from and is none other than stainlessness, which itself is reality totally devoid of any of the deluded apparatus of samsaric mind. Samantabhadra comes forth to the disciple as the wisdom (jnana) king. Wisdom is the knower of a buddha's mind.

Tib. 'char ba. "Shines forth" is a specific term that means that something dawns in mind; comes forth into mind. There are other terms like this but most imply dualistic perception of whatever dawns; this term does not. It is an important term in the higher tantras because of this and hence it is translated in a way that allows you to distinguish it from other types of appearance that comes into mind.

36. Tib. rnam dag. Complete purity is a technical term that appears throughout the sutras and tantras but which has been inconsistently translated and whose meaning will not be obvious to most readers. Complete purity is the specific term for the enlightened aspect of any being's mind. It is complete purity because it is either the potential for the absence of all obscurations in a sentient being's mind or is the actual complete purity of a buddha compared to the obscured, impure state of a sentient being's mind.

37. In other words, the disciple's innate, complete purity appears as the true state of concepts, the king of concepts.

38. Enlightenment's essence is the tathagatagarbha also known as the sugatagarbha; it shines forth as the great bliss of enlightenment.

39. Tib. bdag nyid. Personage means the being of mind, who or what it is.

40. The dharmata's rigpa—its knowing—taken to completion by the practitioner, is Great Completion. The vehicle that comes into our world because of that reality is the supreme vehicle of Great

Completion. That vehicle is king over and subsumes all lesser vehicles.

"That shows each without mixup" refers back two lines to "all things are the equality king that rules over all". It rules over all so its knower, the dharmadhatu rigpa, knows or sees every single thing, just as it is, but does so without mixing up any of the individual items. It knows all but without any blurriness at all.

41. All of the vehicles, from bottom to top, not missing out any, everything included.

42. In other words, may you obtain the result of this empowerment which is that you become a king who has ascended the throne of rulership of the highest level of the view because of the supreme empowerment that is not just any supreme empowerment but the supreme empowerment of this level, the one of true universality.

43. "Dharmata Great Completion" is one of several epithets for Great Completion; it just emphasizes that it is really the dharmata level.

44. Fact here does not mean abstract fact but the actual thing that is present to the mind.

45. Tib. dgongs pa. "Intent" is simply the honorific for mind.

46. Each of the four empowerments starts with a verse and then has a following prose section which expands on the verse, making it a little clearer.

47. Tib. 'od gsal. This has been mistakenly translated as "clear light" for a long time now. In recent times it has also been translated as "lucidity" but this is also an error. The Tibetan exactly translates the Sanskrit "prabhasvara" meaning the illumination that comes from something and which illuminates, that is, the luminosity of

some light source. The buddha used it as a metaphor for the illuminative quality of mind, that is, it is a term pointing to the knowing quality of mind.

48. Self-illumination is the how the luminosity of mind functions in the non-dualistic case; it does not illuminate something other than itself; rather, it illuminates itself and that is what it knows. In other words, the essence of mind knows itself, not something projected as other.

49. Tib. mtshan ma. Conceptual tokens is a specific, technical term that refers to the conceptual structures that are the basis of dualistic perception. In other words, it is saying, "In a non-dualistic mind where there are none of the dualistic things or their sub-conscious, perceptual supports, that is, in luminosity which does not engage in concepts or the distractions belonging to them ...".

50. See the earlier footnote about fact.

51. Expressions, according to Sanskrit and Tibetan grammar following it, are either mental or verbal. Thus, although this is often translated as "word, thought, and expression" it does not mean that; it means expressions, which can be either word or thought (and there is no other possibility).

52. If you pour water onto well-kneaded dough, it either just sits there, not doing anything or runs off the dough. The image is that nothing gets produced, even though something is happening.

53. Tib. gdengs. This term means assurance, not confidence. Note the difference between assurance and confidence.

54. See foremost instructions in the glossary.

55. When all phenomena are without the contrivances of dualistic mind, the complete purity of mind—the tathagatagarbha freed of

all the muck of ignorance and its conceptual paraphernalia—is manifest. That complete purity is at core empty and has a nature of luminosity, that is, a nature that knows. The luminosity functioning as a knower at the fruition level is called wisdom. Wisdom is not like the things of the conceptual domain for it arises in and of itself, without needing any causes or conditions for its existence. Moreover, in this case, it is not something that the disciple has to come up with by searching for intellectually but which has become present as part of the equipoise on the non-dualistic realm that the disciple has just entered through the master's blessings.

This unsought, self-arising wisdom is the equipoise itself of both master and disciple. That equipoise is not a mere, blank knowing but is the wisdom knowing all things. All these dharmas that it knows do not come into existence in the process of cause and effect of the dualistic realm but come into existence in the process, as it is called, of spontaneously existing dharmakaya's realm. This display of the empty-yet-full dharmakaya is the fact being directly perceived by master and disciple.

For a disciple on the path, the fruition wisdom being discussed here is given the special name "rigpa" which translates the Sanskrit "vidya". It does not mean "awareness" but means the very dynamic and alive *knower that has the sight of* both emptiness and its concomitant, uncontrived phenomena. The rigpa itself is the knower. The knower has the capacity for a display of phenomena. This capacity—whether it is merely the capacity or whether it is the capacity actually functioning as a display—is called the liveliness of the rigpa. It is not the expression of the rigpa but the expressivity of the rigpa; the ability to have a display, whether the ability is in effect or not. Therefore, this is the empowerment not merely of the rigpa but of the liveliness of the rigpa, which is tantamount to the dharmakaya as a fully functioning, dynamic state.

Yamantaka is the body aspect of the eight logos and, as such, the empowerment focusses very much on the bodily connection to enlightenment. Therefore, in the preceding empowerments, and especially in the secret empowerment, there has been a great emphasis on the purification of the body constituents as the path to enlightenment. The bodhichitta has a subtle body constituent. This, this supreme empowerment of suchness—the ultimate empowerment of the outer, inner, secret, and suchness empowerments—is connected here with the bodhichitta. Earlier empowerments have also been bodhichitta empowerments but this one is a bodhichitta empowerment of the highest level of view, therefore it is called the Great Completion bodhichitta empowerment.

At this point, the master has led the disciple into this state of wisdom in a way that follows on from the previous empowerments and which has the specific emphases of Yamantaka as a yidam. The master then makes the wish that the disciples actually have this empowerment come to them completely, in full.

Having granted the empowerment in verse, the master then introduces the disciple to the fact of this wisdom in prose.

56. Wisdom can be both the actual wisdom present within yourself as your nature, co-emergent wisdom and the likeness of that actual wisdom which is produced through the bliss-melting practices connected with the earlier empowerments. The master instructs the student to understand that the similitude wisdom introduced in the earlier empowerments is none other than the actual nature, the co-emergent wisdom present within yourself. That wisdom is empty, that is, it is like space. It is ineffable; it cannot be expressed

in word or thought. Nonetheless, the liveliness of the knowing factor of the wisdom does come forth as the display of the wisdom; it comes out as the whole variety of appearances that can and do occur. When it comes out in that display, it is the five wisdoms on display. The essence of the five wisdoms is emptiness yet, despite that, it still appears, totally unhindered by the emptiness factor, as the whole variety of appearances. Moreover, those five wisdoms are not merely empty and capable of going on display as the whole variety of appearances, but they are the primordial state of your being. The master instructs the disciples in how the various aspects of our nature, wisdom, are none other than the five aspects of enlightenment that are, from the beginning, primordially present within us. This is the great liberation that comes because of the primordial reality of your being and which shines forth of itself, that is, which does not need any dualistic causes or conditions for it to be present, doing what it does.

57. Then, as it says in the text, the master should add more, because the text of the empowerment as it has been passed down does not contain a full introduction to mind.

58. Rabjam Rinpoche explained that this can be taken as a reference to both of Dilgo Khyentse Rinpoche's two main gurus, Zhechen Gyaltshab and Dzongsar Khyentse.

59. Rabjam Rinpoche explained that while it is all right not to be a big person with a big name or with large projects such as monasteries, and so on, it is not all right to fall to the other extreme and sink into faint-heartedness.

60. Tib. rtsal. Liveliness has been discussed in a number of other notes. It means the energy of the innate aspect of mind that comes out in various ways, such as discursive thought. Note the threads of meaning in relation to liveliness that run throughout this

composition.

61. Tib. gshis. The basic disposition means the innate character of your being, your most basic disposition, which is another name for the actuality of your own mind. Again, note the thread that runs throughout.

62. Atisha's text on mind training. Rabjam Rinpoche explains that, even though the basic state of mind has been recognized, we still need to train, and what better way to do it than through the bodhichitta mind trainings of Atisha? Train your mind in this, then make prayers of aspiration based on the love and compassion developed and, in terms of recitations of prayers of aspiration, reciting Samantabhadra's well-known prayer of aspiration, *King of Prayers, The Good Conduct* will be excellent.

63. Samantabhadra's well-known prayer of aspiration, *King of Prayers, The Good Conduct*.

64. In these later, degenerate times, we only have the dregs of the five great qualities of life of those humans who lived in the earlier, golden ages.

65. Confusion here means the confusion of sentient beings in general, which is that they see what is not as what is and in so doing, do not see what is, reality, as it is.

66. By taming your own mind, all dharmas, including the bad situations of these degenerate times, will be tamed.

67. Mind's appearances have no intrinsic existence, still they do appear vividly and that very appearance is the complexion of the luminosity aspect of mind. When that is not-stopped, that is, when you do not fall into extremes of emptiness or appearance while practising it, it becomes the transparency of all phenomena known to a

practitioner.

68. Such as the ones just mentioned of how to rest the mind in its own actuality ...

69. Preserve is a technical term meaning to maintain or keep the basic disposition without losing it to distraction.

70. No matter which way the liveliness of mind is expressed, send all of it into self-liberation.

71. Mind's liveliness comes out as appearances and if you steer yourself outwardly towards those, you will fall back into dualistic mind with all the problems mentioned earlier. Do not do that, instead steer inwards, towards the basic disposition, the actuality of mind. If you practice at that, you will one day, come to the finish of the practice of that basic disposition, and at that time, the basic disposition will have become the fruition, dharmakaya. Dilgo Khyentse offers the prayer that the person to whom he is writing the letter will attain to that state, which is the state of Samantabhadra and Samantabhadri undifferentiated. Note also the several threads of male and female woven into this composition, making a very beautiful piece of advice with great depth.

GLOSSARY

Actuality, Tib. gnas lugs: A key term in both sutra and tantra and one of a pair of terms, the other being apparent reality (Tib. snang lugs). The two terms are used when determining the reality of a situation. The actuality of any given situation is how the situation actuality sits or is present; the apparent reality is how any given situation appears to an observer. Something could appear in many different ways, depending on the circumstances at the time and on the being perceiving it but, regardless of those circumstances, it will always have its own actuality, how it really is. The term actuality is frequently used in Mahāmudrā and Great Completion teachings to mean the fundamental reality of any given phenomenon or situation before any deluded mind alters it and makes it appear differently.

Alpha purity, Tib. ka dag: A Great Completion term meaning purity that is there from the first, that is, primordial purity. There are many terms in Buddhism that express the notion of "primordial purity" but this one is unique to the Great Completion teaching. Some people do not like the term "alpha purity" but this is exactly what the Tibetan says.

Assurance, Tib. gdeng: Although often translated as confidence, this term means assurance with all of the extra meaning conveyed by that term. A bird might be confident of its ability to fly but more than that, it has the assurance that it will not fall to the ground because of knowing that it has wings and the training to use them. Similarly, a person might be confident that they could liberate the afflictions but not assured of doing so because of lack of training or other causes. However, a person who has accumulated the causes to be able to liberate afflictions trained is assured of the ability to do so.

Clarity or Illumination, Skt. vara, Tib. gsal ba: When you see this term, it should be understood as an abbreviation of the full term in Tibetan, 'od gsal ba, which is usually translated as luminosity. It is not another factor of mind distinct from luminosity but merely a convenient abbreviation in both Indian and Tibetan dharma language for the longer term, luminosity. See "Luminosity" in this glossary for more.

Complexion, Tib. mdangs: In both Mahāmudrā and Great Completion there is the general term "offput" (Tib. gdangs) meaning what is given off by something, for example the sound given off by a loudspeaker. There is another Tibetan word spelled "mdangs" instead of "gdangs". The Mahāmudrā teaching makes no difference between the two terms but Great Completion teachings does make a distinction. In great completion this term spelled "mdangs" has the special meaning not of the general output or offput coming from something but of the "complexion" of thing. It is a more subtle meaning. In Great Completion it conveys not just the sense of what is given off by the emptiness factor of mind in general (which would be its offput and which is talked about, too) but specifically means the complexion of the emptiness or, you could also say, its lustre.

Conceptual tokens, Tib. mtshan ma. Conceptual tokens are the actual structures or concepts that conceptual mind uses during the process of perception. For example, you could see a table in direct visual perception of table in which case there would be no conceptual tokens involved. Or, you could think "table" in a conceptual perception of table in which case there is a always a name-tag "table" used whenever the table is referenced. The name tag is the conceptual token. This term is often used in Buddhist literature as way of inferring that the process of mind being discussed is not one of non-dualistic wisdom but one of dualistic mind.

Confusion, Tib. 'khrul pa: In Buddhism, this term mostly refers to the fundamental confusion of taking things the wrong way that happens because of fundamental ignorance though it can also have the more general meaning of having lots of thoughts and being confused about it. In the first case, it is defined like this, "Confusion is the appearance to rational mind of something being present when it is not", and refers for example to seeing an object, such as a table, as being truly present when in fact it is present only as mere, interdependent appearance.

Contrivance, contrived, Tib. bcos pa: A term meaning that something has been altered from its native state.

Cyclic existence, Skt. saṃsāra, Tib. 'khor ba: The type of existence that sentient beings have which is that they continue on from one existence to another, always within the enclosure of births that are produced by ignorance and experienced as unsatisfactory. Although the Tibetan term literally means "cycling", the original Sanskrit has a slightly different meaning; it means to go about, here and there.

Dharmakaya, Tib. chos sku: The mind of a buddha. Dharma here means reality, what actually is, and kāya means body.

Dharmata, Tib. chos nyid: A Sanskrit term used to refer to the reality of any given situation. Thus, there are many dharmatās. The term is often used in Buddhism to refer to general reality that underlies all types of existence but that is not its only meaning. For example, even the fact of water's wetness can be referred to as the dharmatā of water, meaning water's reality in general. The term is similar to "actuality" (Tib. gnas lugs).

Direct Crossing, Tib. tho rgal: The name of the two main practices of the innermost level of Great Completion. The other one is Thorough Cut.

Discursive thought, Skt. vikalpita, Tib. rnam rtog: This means more than just the superficial thought that is heard as a voice in the head. It includes the entirety of conceptual process that arises due to mind contacting any object of any of the senses. The Sanskrit and Tibetan literally mean "(dualistic) thought (that arises from the mind wandering among the) various (superficies perceived in the doors of the senses)".

Elaboration, Tib. spro ba: to be producing thoughts.

Entity, Tib. ngo bo: The entity of something is just exactly what that thing is. In English we would often simply say "thing" rather than entity but there is the problem that, in Buddhism, "thing" has a very specific meaning and not the general meaning that it has in English. See also under Essence in this glossary.

Equipoise and post-attainment, Tib. mnyam bzhag and rjes thob: Although often called "meditation and post-meditation", the actual term is "equipoise and post-attainment". There is great meaning in the actual wording which is lost by the looser translation.

Essence, Tib. ngo bo: This is a key term used throughout Buddhist theory. The original in Sanskrit and the term in Tibetan, too, has both meanings of "essence" and "entity". In some situations the term has more the first meaning and in others, the second. For example, when speaking of mind and mind's essence, it is referring to the core or essential part within mind. On the other hand, when speaking of something such as fire, one can speak of the entity, fire, and its characteristics, such as heat, and so on; in this case, the term does not mean essence but means that thing, what is actually is.

Fictional, Skt. saṃvṛti, Tib. kun rdzob: This term is paired with the term "superfactual" q.v. Until now these two terms have been translated as "relative" and "absolute" but the translations are nothing like the original terms. These terms are extremely important in the Buddhist teaching so it is very important that they be corrected but more than that, if the actual meaning of these terms is not presented, then the teaching connected with them cannot be understood.

The Sanskrit term saṃvṛti means a deliberate invention, a fiction, a hoax. It refers to the mind of ignorance which, because of being obscured and so not seeing suchness, is not true but a fiction. The things that appear to the ignorance are therefore fictional. Nonetheless, the beings who live in this ignorance believe that the things that appear to them through the filter of ignorance are true, are real. Therefore, these beings live in fictional truth.

Fictional truth, Skt. saṃvṛtisatya, Tib. kun rdzob bden pa: See under "Fictional" for an explanation of this term.

Foremost instruction, Skt. upadeśha, Tib. man ngag: there are several types of instruction mentioned in Buddhist literature: there is the general level of instruction which is the meaning contained in the words of the texts of the tradition; on a more personal and direct level there is oral instruction which has been passed down from teacher to student from the time of the buddha; and on the most profound level there is upadeśha which are not only oral instructions provided by one's guru but are special, core instructions that come out of personal experience and which convey the teaching concisely and with the full weight of personal experience. Upadeśha are crucial to the Vajra Vehicle because these are the special way of passing on the profound instructions needed for the student's realization.

Grasped-grasping, Tib. gzung 'dzin: When mind is turned outwardly as it is in the normal operation of dualistic mind, it has developed two faces that appear simultaneously. Special names are given to these two faces: mind appearing in the form of the external object being referenced is called "that which is grasped". Mind appearing in the form of the consciousness that is referencing it is called "the grasper" or "grasping" of it. Thus, there is the pair of terms "grasped-grasper" or "grasped-grasping". When these two terms are used, it alerts you immediately to the fact that a Mind Only style of presentation is being discussed. This pair of terms pervades Mind Only, Madhyamaka, and tantric writings and is exceptionally important in all of them.

Note that you could substitute the word "apprehended" for "grasped" and "apprehender" for "grasper" or "grasping" and that would reflect one connotation of the original Indian terminology. The solidified duality of grasped and grasper is nothing but an invention of dualistic thought. It has that kind of character or characteristic.

Ground, Tib. gzhi: This is the first member of the formulation of ground, path, and fruition. Ground, path, and fruition is the way that the teachings of the path of oral instruction belonging to the Vajra Vehicle are presented to students. Ground refers to the basic situation as it is.

Intent, Tib. dgongs pa: The honorific term for the way that something is understood or for a mind that has a certain understanding.

Introduction and To Introduce, Tib. ngos sprad and ngos sprod pa respectively: This pair of terms is usually translated in the U.S.A. these days as "pointing out" "and "to point out" but this is a mistake that has, unfortunately, become entrenched. The terms are the standard terms used in day to day life for the situation in which one person introduces another person to someone or something. They are the exact same words as our English "introduction" and "to introduce".

In the Vajra Vehicle, these terms are specifically used for the situation in which one person introduces another person to the nature of his own mind. Now there is a term in Tibetan for "pointing out" but that term is never used for this purpose because in this case no-one points out anything. Rather, a person is introduced by another person to a part of himself that he has forgotten about.

Key points, Tib. gnad: Key points are those places in one's being that one works, like pressing buttons, in order to get some desired effect. For example, in meditation, there are key points of the body; by adjusting those key points, the mind is brought closer to reality and the meditation is thus assisted.

In general, this term is used in Buddhist meditation instruction but it is, in particular, part of the special vocabulary of the Great Completion teachings. Overall, the Great Completion teachings are given as a series of key points that must be attended to in order to bring forth the various realizations of the path.

Liveliness, Tib. rtsal: A key term in both Mahāmudrā and Great Completion. The term means the ability that something has to express itself. In the case of rigpa, it refers to how the rigpa actually comes out into expression. The term is sometimes translated as "display" but that is not right. It is not merely the display that is being talked about here but the fact that something has the ability to express itself in a certain way. Another English word that fits the meaning, though one which is drier than "liveliness" is "expressivity". In the end, given the way that this term is actually used in the higher tantras, it refers to the liveliness of whatever is being referred to, usually rigpa.

Luminosity, Skt. prabhāsvara, Tib. 'od gsal ba: the core of mind, called mind's essence, has two aspects, parts, or factors as they are called. One is emptiness and the other is knowing. Luminosity is a metaphor for the fundamental knowing quality of the essence of mind. It is sometimes translated as "clear light" but that is a mistake that comes from not understanding how the words of the Sanskrit and the Tibetan, too, go together. It does not refer to a light that has the quality of clearness (something that makes no sense, actually!) but refers to the illuminative property which is the hallmark of mind. Mind knows, that is what it does. Metaphorically, it is a luminosity that illuminates its own content. In both Sanskrit and Tibetan Buddhist literature, the term is frequently abbreviated just to gsal ba, "clarity", with the same meaning.

Mind, Skt. chitta, Tib. sems: the complicated process of mind which occurs because there is ignorance. This sort of mind is a samsaric phenomenon. It is a dualistic mind.

Mindness, Skt. chittatā, Tib. sems nyid. Mindness is a specific term of the tantras. It is one of many terms meaning the essence of mind or the nature of mind. It conveys the sense of "what mind is at its very core". It has sometimes been translated as "mind itself" but that is a misunderstanding of the Tibetan word "nyid". The term does not mean "that thing mind" where mind refers to dualistic mind. Rather, it means the very core of dualistic mind, what mind is at root, without all of the dualistic baggage.

Mindness is a path term. It refers to exactly the same thing as "actuality" or "actuality of mind" which is a ground term but does so from the practitioner's perspective. It conveys the sense to a practitioner that he might still have baggage of dualistic mind that has not been purified yet but there is a core to that mind that he can work with.

Not stopped, Tib. ma 'gags pa: An important path term in the teaching of both Mahāmudrā and Great Completion. The essence of mind has two parts: emptiness and luminosity. Both of these must come unified. However, when a practitioner does the practice, he will fall into one extreme or the other and that is called "stoppage". The aim of the practice is to get to the stage in which there is both emptiness and luminosity together. In that case, there is no stoppage of falling into one extreme or the other. Thus non-stopped luminosity is a term that indicates that there is the luminosity with all of its appearance yet that luminosity, for the practitioner, is not mistaken, is not stopped off. Stopped luminosity is an experience like luminosity but in which the appearances have, at least to some extent, not been mixed with emptiness.

Post-attainment, Tib. rjes thob: See "Equipoise and post-attainment".

Preserve, Tib. skyong ba: An important term in both Mahāmudrā and Great Completion. In general, it means to defend, protect, nurture, maintain. In the higher tantras it means to keep something just as it is, to nurture that something so that it stays and is not lost. Also, in the higher tantras, it is often used in reference to preserving the state where the state is some particular state of being. Because of this, the phrase "preserve the state" is an important instruction in the higher tantras.

Proliferation, Tib. 'phro ba: A term meaning that the dualistic mind has become active and is giving off thoughts. This is actually the same word as "elaboration" but is the intransitive sense.

Rational mind, Tib. blo: The Kagyu and Nyingma traditions use this term pejoratively for the most part. In the Great Completion and Mahāmudrā teachings, this term specifically means the dualistic mind. It is the villain, so to speak, which needs to be removed from the equation in order to obtain enlightenment. This term is commonly translated simply as mind but that causes confusion with the many other words that are also translated simply as mind. It is not just another mind but is specifically the sort of mind that creates the situation of this and that (ratio in Latin) and hence upholds the duality of samsara. It is the very opposite of the essence of mind. Thus, this is a key term which should be noted and not just glossed over as "mind".

Rigpa, Tib. rig pa: This is the singularly most important term in the whole of Great Completion and Mahāmudrā. In particular, it is the key word of all words in the Great Completion system of the Thorough Cut. Rigpa literally means to know in the sense of "I see!" It is used at all levels of meaning from the coarsest everyday sense of knowing something to the deepest sense of knowing something as presented in the system of Thorough Cut. The system of Thorough Cut uses this term in a very special sense, though it still retains its basic meaning of "to know". To translate it as "awareness" which is common practice these days is a poor practice; there are many kinds of awareness but there is only one rigpa and besides, rigpa is substantially more than just awareness. Since this is such an important term and since it lacks an equivalent in English, I choose not to translate it. However, it will be helpful in reading the text to understanding the meaning as just given.

This is the term used to indicate enlightened mind as experienced by the practitioner on the path of these practices. The term itself specifically refers to the dynamic knowing quality of mind. It absolutely does not mean a simple registering, as implied by the word "awareness" which unfortunately is often used to translate this term. There is no word in English that exactly matches it, though the idea of "seeing" or "insight on the spot" is very close. Proof of this is found in the fact that the original Sanskrit term "vidyā" is actually the root of all words in English that start with "vid" and mean "to see", for example, "video", "vision", and so on. Chogyam Trungpa Rinpoche, who was particular skilled at getting Tibetan words into English, also stated that this term rigpa really did not have a good equivalent in English, though he thought that "insight" was the closest. My own conclusion after hearing extensive teaching on it is that rigpa is just best left untranslated. However, it will be helpful in reading the text to understanding the meaning as just given.

Note that rigpa has both noun and verb forms. To get the verb form, I use "rigpa'ing".

Seat of rulership, Tib. btsan sa: The place at which one has gained total dominion over all else. It is the high place above all others which not only rules over all others but is unassailable by all others. In Great Completion literature, the term is especially used in relation to Thorough Cut practice where it is used as part of the metaphor of attaining to the governing position of re-connecting to one's innate, primordial reality.

Secret Mantra, Tib. gsang sngags: Another name for the Vajra Vehicle or the tantric teachings.

State, Tib. ngang: A key term in Mahāmudrā and Great Completion. Unfortunately it is often not translated and in so doing much meaning is lost. Alternatively, it is often translated as "within" which is incorrect. The term means a "state". A state is a certain, ongoing situation. In Buddhist meditation in general, there are various states that a practitioner has to enter and remain in as part of developing the meditation.

Superfactual, Skt. paramārtha, Tib. don dam: This term is paired with the term "fictional" q.v. Until now these two terms have been translated as "relative" and "absolute" but those translations are nothing like the original terms. These terms are extremely important in the Buddhist teaching so it is very important that their translations be corrected but, more than that, if the actual meaning of these terms is not presented, the teaching connected with them cannot be understood.

The Sanskrit term parāmartha literally means "a superior or holy kind of fact" and refers to the wisdom mind possessed by those who have developed themselves spiritually to the point of having transcended samsara. That wisdom is *superior* to an ordinary, un-developed person's consciousness and the *facts* that appear on its surface are superior compared to the facts that appear on the ordinary person's consciousness. Therefore, it is superfact or the holy fact, more literally. What this wisdom sees is true for the beings who have it, therefore what the wisdom sees is superfactual truth.

Superfactual truth, Skt. paramārthasatya, Tib. don dam bden pa: see under "Superfactual" for an explanation of this term.

Thorough Cut, Tib. khregs chod: the Dzogchen system has several levels to it. The innermost level has two main practices, the first called Thregcho which literally translates as Thorough Cut and the second called Thogal which translates as Direct Crossing. The meaning of Thorough Cut has been misunderstood. The meaning is clearly explained in the *Illuminator Tibetan-English Dictionary*:

> "Thorough Cut is a practice in which the solidification that sentient beings produce by having rational minds which grasp at a perceived object and perceiving subject is sliced through so as to get the underlying reality which has always been present in the essence of mind and which is called Alpha Purity in this system of teachings. For this reason, Thorough Cut is also known as Alpha Purity Thorough Cut."

The etymology of the word is explained in the Great Completion teachings either as ཁྲེགས་སུ་ཆོད་པ་ or ཁྲེགས་གོ་ཆོད་པ་. In either case, the term ཆོད་པ་ is "a cut"; there are all sorts of different "cuts" and this is one of them. Then, in the case of ཁྲེགས་སུ་ཆོད་པ་, ཁྲེགས་ སུ་ is an adverb modifying the verb "to cut" and has the meaning of making the cut fully, completely. It is explained with the example of slicing off a finger. A finger could be sliced with a sharp knife such that the cut was not quite complete and the cut off portion was left hanging. Alternatively, it could be sliced through in one, decisive movement such that the finger was completely and definitely severed. That kind of thorough cut is what is meant here. In the case of ཁྲེགས་གི་ཆོད་པ, the term ཁྲེགས་གི is as an adverb that has the meaning of something that is doubtless, of something that is unquestionably so. A translation based on the first explanation would be "Thorough Cut" and on the second would be "Decisive Cut".

Other translations that have been put forward for this term are: "Cutting Resistance" and "Cutting Solidity". Of these, "Cutting Resistance" is usually a translation made on the basis of students expressing the "resistance to practice", etcetera. That is a complete misunderstanding of the term. The term means that that the practitioner of this system cuts *decisively* through rational mind, regardless of its degree of solidity, so as to arrive directly at the essence of mind.

Three principal trainings, Tib. bslabs pa gsum: The three principal trainings of the Buddhist path are shīla, samādhi, and prajñā— discipline, concentration, and correct discernment.

Three secrets, Tib. gsang ba: This is a path term which refers to the body, speech, and mind of a person who is on the way to buddhahood. When the person becomes a buddha, they have reached their full state of enlightenment so are then referred to as the three vajras of a tathāgata. Occasionally this path term is used to refer to the body, speech, and mind of a buddha.

Three types of analysis, Tib. dpyad pa gsum: There are three types of inferential reasoning that can be used to assess anything not known with direct perception. One of them is the type of reasoning called Reasoning of the Force of the Thing. The remaining two are the reasoning that relies on the trustworthiness of others who have made statements about the thing being examined and the reasoning that relies on popular knowledge concerning the status of the thing being examined. The first one is superior to the other two. When a thing is examined with all three types of reasoning and it is discerned to be valid, it is said to be "pure" after application of the three reasonings.

Transparency, Tib. zang thal: This term belongs to the unique vocabulary of Great Completion. It has two connotations: that something is seen directly, in direct perception; and that it is seen with full visibility because there is no agent obscuring the view of it. The term is used to indicate that rigpa is truly present for the practitioner. Luminosity when it is the rigpa of the enlightened side and not the not-rigpa, usually translated as ignorance, of the samsaric side, has transparency or, you could say, full visibility, as one of its qualities precisely because it has none of the factors of mind as such in it, which would obscure it. Transparency means that the rigpa is in full view: it really is rigpa seen in direct perception and it is without rational mind so it is seen without any of the obscuring factors that would make it less than immediately and fully visible.

Unaltered or uncontrived, Tib. ma bcos pa: The opposite of "altered" and "contrived". Something which has not been altered from its native state; something which has been left just as it is.

Upadesha, Tib. man ngag: See the glossary entry "Foremost Instruction".

View, meditation, and conduct, Tib. lta sgom spyod: A formulation of the teachings that contains all of the meaning of the path.

Wisdom, Skt. jñāna, Tib. ye shes: This is a fruition term that refers to the kind of mind, the kind of knower possessed by a buddha. The original Sanskrit term has many meanings but overall has the sense of just knowing. In Buddhism, it refers to the most basic type of knowing possible. Sentient beings could do this but their minds are obscured so, although they have the potential for knowing with the wisdom of a buddha, it does not happen. If they practise the path to buddhahood, at some point they will leave behind their obscuration and start knowing in this very simple and immediate way.

This sort of knowing is there at the core of every being's mind. Therefore, the Tibetans called it "the particular type of awareness which is always there". Because of their wording, it is often called "primordial wisdom" but that is too much. It simply means wisdom in the sense of the most fundamental knowing possible.

INDEX